D1035265

Lincolnshire

A PORTRAIT IN COLOUR

ROD EDWARDS &
JEZ ASHBERRY

COUNTRYSIDE BOOKS

Other counties in this series include:

BUCKINGHAMSHIRE	DORSET	SUFFOLK
CHESHIRE	ESSEX	SURREY
DERBYSHIRE	HAMPSHIRE	SUSSEX
DEVON	LEICESTERSHIRE	WARWICKSHIRE

For Rosemary

First published 1998
© Photographs, Rod Edwards 1998
© Text, Jez Ashberry 1998

COUNTRYSIDE BOOKS
3 CATHERINE ROAD
NEWBURY, BERKSHIRE

ISBN 1 85306 527 7

The photograph on page 1 shows the beach at Mablethorpe.
The photograph on page 5 was taken near Aswardy, Sleaford.

Designed by Mon Mohan
Produced through MRM Associates Ltd, Reading
Printed in Singapore

Contents

INTRODUCTION

Lincolnshire is England's second largest county, and yet precious few outsiders seem to know very much about this region of unsurpassed variety. There are good reasons for this. To the best of my knowledge it has never been the setting for a television series harking back to a more innocent age; it is not an area much visited by tourists; its people do not pop up in the media, as do Geordies, Scousers and Tykes, to present us with a stereotypical image of themselves and their native county.

No: Lincolnshire is famously, gloriously obscure, and that is the way most Lincolnshire yellowbellies like it – they keep themselves to themselves, and by and large they expect everyone else to do likewise. The best efforts of marketing officers to encourage holidaymakers to do more than pay a token, once-a-year visit to Skegness, the gaudy queen of the Lincolnshire coast, are mostly viewed with scepticism by the locals. For Lincolnshire is one of those rare things: a genuinely undiscovered county. And most Lincolnshire folk are cautious about sharing it with anyone else.

If Kent is the garden of England, then Lincolnshire is its allotment. It is certainly a place in thrall to the farmers – and not in a sleepy, haywain-and-duckpond sort of a way, either. Great tracts of the county are given over to the most intensive, industrially driven agriculture this country has ever known. Where once there were sheep and potatoes, now there is virtually every cash-rich crop under the sun: if you ever put carrots, cabbage or cauliflower on your plate, the chances are they've been grown in the fabulously fertile soil of Lincolnshire.

But there is, of course, much more to my home county than that – there has to be in an area which stretches 80 miles from the Humber Bridge in the north (the gateway to Hull and the Yorkshire Wolds) to Stamford in the south (a town within easy commuting distance of London).

We could indeed begin our tour of Lincolnshire at Stamford, a town of such architectural merit that it was made Britain's first conservation area in 1967. Or we could start at Lincoln, formerly a Roman *colonia* of some standing and now home to what has been called the grandest Gothic cathedral in Europe. Or we could set out from Boston, capital of the Lincolnshire fens, first taking in the view from the tower of St Botolph's church (its steeple is the tallest in the country), which reveals the enormity of the effort required to drain these great swamps. Or we could choose another ecclesiastical prodigy – St James's church in Louth, which has one of the most famous spires in England – and from there survey the tranquil folds and valleys that inspired Tennyson.

In between there is a wealth of history and an expanse of unspoilt countryside that will charm the visitors who come here. There are tidy market towns by the dozen, neat stone-and-pantile villages and hardy little fenland hamlets; there are dykes (ditches) and windmills, grand country houses, fields of daffodils, pockets of industry, green fields, blue skies, and a truly phenomenal array of ancient churches. Begin and conclude your tour wherever you choose; by the end of it you will be the richer for your knowledge of a little-known county and the poorer for shoe leather.

Jez Ashberry

Stamford

The name of Daniel Lambert, the heaviest man England has ever known, lives on in Stamford. The local football team is nicknamed the Daniels and the popular Daniel Lambert pub stands near the town centre in St Leonard's Street – and if you want to get an impression of how big a 52-stone man really is, then you can see a replica set of his clothes on display at the town's museum.

It was mere chance that connected Lambert with Stamford. A native of Leicester, he came to see the Stamford races in 1809 and collapsed and died while staying at the Waggon and Horses Inn. His body was put into an outsized coffin and rolled on two axles and four wheels into a sloping grave in St Martin's churchyard – though not before the window and part of the wall in his room had been removed to get the coffin out.

General Tom Thumb, the celebrated American midget, was as interested as anyone to compare his size with that of Lambert. While visiting Stamford in 1846 he dropped into the London Inn on St John's Street to view a suit of Lambert's clothes, and he left a suit of his own so that future visitors might make a comparison (*inset*).

But such freaks of nature are incidental to the fame of Stamford (*opposite*), dubbed 'England's most attractive town' by John Betjeman. The novelist Sir Walter Scott spoke for many admirers when he described St Mary's Hill as 'the finest scene between London and Edinburgh'. Stamford is one of those rare towns of great age, harmony and beauty, at once well preserved – it was made Britain's first conservation area in 1967 – and full of life.

Scott was not the only literary figure to have had his imagination stirred by Stamford's beauty: Anthony Trollope is widely thought to have taken his inspiration for *The Warden*, one of his 'Barchester Chronicles', from Browne's Hospital, the 15th-century almshouses which now house occasional exhibitions as well as elderly residents in a sympathetic Victorian extension of 1870.

And if all that still isn't enough, try a visit to one of Stamford's five medieval churches, to its steam brewery museum or to its serene meadows, where the river Welland makes its idle way towards its outfall in the Wash. One can only agree with the intrepid 17th-century traveller Celia Fiennes, who wrote that Stamford is 'as fine a built town all of stone as may be seen'.

Burghley House

Hermann Goering, chief of the German Luftwaffe during the Second World War, knew the importance of Burghley House (*opposite and inset*). 'Burghley is mine,' he growled by way of ordering his bomber crews to avoid this jewel just outside Stamford. Goering planned to use Burghley as his country cottage after the successful Nazi invasion of Great Britain. But what a cottage! Burghley has been described as 'the largest and grandest house of the first Elizabethan age', and its interior ranks alongside some of England's best-stocked art galleries.

There are those who will argue that Burghley has no place in a book on Lincolnshire, since most of the estate now lies within the boundaries of Cambridgeshire. But that is a cartographer's quibble: Burghley has been linked with Stamford since the 16th century, when David Cecil bought it and William Cecil, the first Lord Burghley and later Queen Elizabeth I's Chief Secretary, set about enlarging and improving it.

Today it is home to Lady Victoria Leatham (of *Antiques Roadshow* fame), the daughter of David Cecil, the sixth Marquess of Exeter, an Olympic gold medallist portrayed by Nigel Havers in the film *Chariots of Fire*. It is also home to one of the finest collections of 17th-century Italian art to be found anywhere in the world, and every September it becomes the focal point for horse-lovers everywhere: the Burghley Horse Trials were first staged on the estate in 1960, when the last Lord Burghley agreed to allow the British Horse Society to move its autumn horse trials from Harewood House in Yorkshire.

A highlight in the equestrian calendar, the Burghley Horse Trials combine showjumping, dressage and cross-country with such distractions as dog agility competitions and some very high-brow shopping opportunities. And all this is played out in front of one of England's grandest stately homes. How lucky we are that Goering never got his hands on it …

Spalding

If you woke up one day and found yourself in Spalding you could be forgiven for believing that you'd been whisked over the sea to Holland. Here are long and elegant terraces of Georgian town houses lining the banks of the river Welland, wide, flat countryside surrounding the town (*inset*), and tulips in abundance – at least, for part of the year.

So ubiquitous was the tulip when Spalding's bulb industry was in its prime that the flower became the symbol of both South Holland District Council (with its base in Spalding) and BBC Radio Lincolnshire. Even Spalding's football team chose 'the Tulips' as its nickname.

But visitors making the long journey through the fens to see the tulip fields in glorious, blazing colour could now be disappointed: from a peak in 1939, when over 100,000 acres of fields around Spalding were given over to tulip

cultivation, fewer than 200 acres now remain (*opposite*). Tulips do not take kindly to modern mechanised methods of farming, and much of the tulip growing in Lincolnshire today goes on out of sight of the motorist.

The town's annual tulip festival survives, however, showing off enough colourful flower heads to satisfy even the most ardent enthusiast. Bulb growing has been part of life in Spalding for over a century, but the May festival and its famous flower parade, with its floats bedecked with tulip heads, was first held as recently as 1959.

If the sight of millions of tulips still leaves you hungry for more, then there's only one thing for it: a trip to the tulip museum in nearby Pinchbeck, set up in order to record the passing of an industry which once gave employment to thousands of local men, women and children.

Crowland

Crowland, the remotest outpost of the Lincolnshire fens, has a very special character. It was the bleakness and dreariness of this desolate island in the swamps that tempted St Guthlac, patron saint of the fens, to settle here in AD 699 and begin a life of penitential hardship after years of soldiering. Though it has since been civilised, Crowland remains an eerie and isolated little town.

The son of a Mercian nobleman, Guthlac gave up his warlike ways at the age of 25 and chose a monk's life instead, studying for two years at the monastery at Repton in Yorkshire. But even that austere existence was too comfortable for him, and he resolved to sail out into the fens of Lincolnshire with his boatman, Tatwin, and found a hermitage wherever his boat became stranded. Croyland was that place (the spelling of its name, meaning 'muddy land', has been altered by mistake); according to the carved quatrefoil over the west door of the abbey nave, the only inhabitants of the place were a sow and her litter of piglets.

Crowland is dominated today by the looming wreck of the Benedictine abbey which was founded in 716, two years after Guthlac's death. Fire, earthquake and Viking raids struck in succession, but each time the abbey rose, as if by a miracle, out of the watery waste. The present building (*opposite*), which dates from the 14th and 15th centuries, was partly demolished at the time of the dissolution of the monasteries and further damaged by a Parliamentarian bombardment in 1643. Much of the stone was then carted off to build houses in Crowland, but the north aisle of the abbey is still used as the town's parish church, and the ruined west front gives visitors a clear idea of the former grandeur of the building.

Crowland is undoubtedly an odd place, and it has an oddity at its centre to match. The unique Triangular or Trinity bridge once spanned the confluence of two streams where the river Welland forked – but when the fens were drained the streams diminished and were eventually covered in. Today the stone bridge stands high and dry in the centre of the town (*inset*) – a bridge to nowhere spanning nothing more than cobblestones. Crowland's quiet streets are unusually broad, and many still feature a grassy strip down the middle where the streams of the river Welland once flowed.

Boston – St Botolph's

The treasure of Boston, and its enduring symbol, is the extraordinary and outsized church of St Botolph (*opposite*) – its prodigious lantern tower overlooking the river Witham, its chancel protruding into the marvellously wide and irregular market-place. 'Boston Stump', as the locals call it, is my favourite of all buildings, and yet whenever I am in my home town I have to force myself to look at it afresh.

St Botolph's is England's fourth largest parish church, and its steeple beats all comers. To understand why such an enormous church was built for what is today a place of only modest size is to gain some insight into Boston's importance in the Middle Ages: levies paid by the town in the 13th century were only slightly less than those paid by London and were larger than those of any other English port. Boston made its fortune exporting wool to the Continent and importing all manner of exotic goods, and the church – begun in 1309 and not completed until more than two centuries later – was a visible expression of Bostonian wealth and ambition.

It is apt that St Botolph's, built right on the river bank, should provide a physical link between the tidal Witham and the market-place, for the church owes its grandeur both to the port and to the market, which has been a regular feature of Boston life since 1308. And you don't have to walk far from this corner of the town to glimpse other important remnants of Boston's history: close to the market-place is a cluster of buildings which provide a snapshot of the town's past (*inset*).

Opposite the former quayside in Spain Lane are the remains of the 13th-century refectory of the Dominican friars, converted in 1965 to become the Blackfriars Arts Centre and theatre at the instigation of local enthusiasts.

A little further south is the Guildhall, once the 15th-century hall of the Guild of St Mary and now the town's small but well stocked museum. Inside are the very cells in which some of the Pilgrim Fathers were imprisoned in 1607 after they were betrayed in their flight to Holland.

The Maud Foster Mill and Fydell House

Boston's recovery from the economic stagnation following the silting-up of its port was hastened in the 18th and 19th centuries, when the programme to drain the watery fens around the town was almost complete, and when long-awaited improvements were made to the river Witham and to the port itself. The engineer Langley Edwards built the first grand sluice to the north of the town in 1764, allowing the freshwater Witham to be held in check at high tide; and Boston's dock basin was cut in 1884 in order to attract larger vessels into the port.

It is on one of the drainage canals characteristic of this part of Lincolnshire that another of Boston's famous landmarks stands: the Maud Foster Mill (*inset*), which overlooks the Maud Foster drain to the north of the town. The drain is old   it was cut in 1568 — and was named after the woman who owned the land through which it was to run. The mill is newer, of course: it was built in 1819 and is one of a handful in England still working and milling flour all year round (Lincolnshire leads the way with three survivors); it is also England's tallest working mill. A five-sailed tower mill with an ogee cap, it was restored to working order in 1988 and is regularly open to the public.

Back in the heart of the town, close to the Guildhall, is more evidence of Boston's 18th-century prosperity: Fydell House (*opposite*), built by an unknown architect in 1726, and the nearby Customs House. Originally built as William Fydell's handsome in-town residence, Fydell House is now Pilgrim College, part of the University of Nottingham's adult education department; and it has recently been licensed for civil weddings, so now you can get married there too.

The Customs House in nearby South Street dates from the same early 18th-century period, a time when Boston was emerging from decay and rediscovering its former confidence. The town was never again to see the great wealth it had known in medieval times, but today's visitors can still learn much about its chequered history.

The Fens

When first-time visitors look upon the endless flat horizons and the enormous skies of the Lincolnshire fenlands they find it difficult to believe that as recently as Roman times much of this landscape was densely wooded.

The fens of eastern England which Lincolnshire shares with Cambridgeshire and Norfolk have been shaped almost single-handedly by man — by both his ingenuity and his neglect. While the Romans occupied this part of Britain they built sea walls and maintained the river outfalls, but when they left, the fenlands suffered a predictable calamity: the sea breached the defences, salt water flooded the low-lying land, river outfalls silted up, and the whole area became a watery waste.

For a thousand years men strove to reclaim the fen, but vested interests and the sheer scale of the task of drainage made progress painfully slow. In the 1640s a man at last stepped forward with a scheme to drain and improve the fens: the eminent Dutch engineer Sir Cornelius Vermuyden began the work which was only completed in the 19th century. By straightening rivers, cutting new drains and pumping the water out to sea — first with windmills, and later with steam engines — the fens were transformed from a dank, misty and malarial wilderness into a fertile plain ideal for cultivation.

Today the most productive farming soil in Britain — some say the entire world — is the dark and gleaming earth of the Lincolnshire fenland. Here are vast farms producing potatoes, sugar beet, flower bulbs (*opposite*) and root vegetables; here are scores of memorable medieval churches, whose spires seem a concrete expression of the ancient desire to drag this land out of the water; here too are the doughty, wind-blasted villages of the fen, their names truly from the back of beyond: Gedney Dyke, Whaplode Drove, Moulton Chapel and Surfleet Seas End.

Only by visiting the fens can one truly appreciate the enormity of the task which faced those engineers and the hardy nature of the people who work the fenland soil today. Drive south from Spalding or Holbeach and you are in the heart of the fens: the road runs ten feet above the level of the land, the wind whips across the fields from over the North Sea, and remote fenland cottages huddle together for comfort. Little allowance is made for the tourist who happens to find himself in the fens, but the Pinchbeck Engine Museum near Spalding tells the story of the colossal struggle to reclaim this part of Lincolnshire from the sea (*inset*).

18

Wrawby Post Mill and the Sibsey Trader Mill

Most of Lincolnshire – with the exception of the wolds – is low-lying country, and its exposed position on the eastern coast of England leaves it open to cold winds which howl across the North Sea from Russia and northern Europe.

It can be chilly, but more often than not the locals can use the elements to their advantage. As early as the 16th century those living in the fens borrowed the Dutch idea of using wind engines to drain their marshy homeland; and even after the invention of the steam pump, the windmill remained the most effective miller of grain.

The two mills featured here were both built to grind corn, but they differ radically in design. Wrawby Mill (*inset*) is Lincolnshire's last surviving post mill, built of wood and designed to rotate on a post in order to catch the wind. No one is absolutely certain when it was built, but its construction seems to indicate a date between 1760 and 1790.

For most of the 20th century the survival of Wrawby Mill has been in doubt – indeed, in 1961 it was saved from demolition by a band of local people who formed a society dedicated to its preservation. Wrawby Mill was renovated and began milling corn in 1965, and today the society which cares for it opens the mill to the public throughout the year.

The Sibsey Trader (*opposite*) is of a more orthodox Lincolnshire design. A brick tower mill standing just outside the village of Sibsey, north of Boston, it was built in 1877 on the site of a post mill by the Louth millwrights John Sanderson and Co. Its name derives from the fact that a group of local farmers acted co-operatively in order to have their corn ground at a reduced price. Like the mill at Wrawby, the Sibsey Trader has been renovated, and now there's even a tearoom for visitors in the shadow of the sails.

Folkingham

'Nobody should hurry through Folkingham,' wrote Henry Thorold, that redoubtable authority on Lincolnshire, in a recent book about the county. Indeed, it is all but impossible for anyone to hurry through this handsome village, for its wholly unexpected charm stops the visitor short.

The best way to approach Folkingham (*opposite*) is from the south, along the A15 from Bourne. Climb the modest rise in the road and you'll be rewarded with a splendid view of the village laid out before you: alongside the pinnacled tower of St Andrew's church is the façade of the

Greyhound Inn, its archway for coaches a clue to the fact that Folkingham was once an important staging post along the road to London; then there is the expansive market-place sloping down towards the south, bordered on either side by fine, unspoiled Georgian houses of two and three storeys; and in the foreground are Folkingham Manor and the gatehouse of the old House of Correction.

Yet Folkingham has not always been such a pleasant place to look upon: in the 17th and 18th centuries, by all accounts, it was filthy and neglected. The Greyhound in those days was described as 'a miserable hovel', with a foul-smelling well outside its door; the passage of many coaches and carts made the main road treacherous, and the sale of livestock on market days created a din and a stink which can scarcely be imagined.

Today's inhabitants of Folkingham have the Heathcote family to thank for the neat and ordered appearance of their village. It was purchased in 1788 for Sir Gilbert, the fourth Baronet Heathcote, as a sound investment for the young man, and his thoughtful relatives even employed an architect to produce a new village plan.

Part of the work to improve Folkingham included the House of Correction which can still be seen today (*inset*); it was built in 1852 to replace the old prison, which now serves as two residential houses in the market-place. There is indeed no need to hurry through Folkingham, for the grim-looking gatehouse – the only part of the gaol to survive – is now owned by the Landmark Trust, and you can rent it as a base for holidays if you wish.

Grimsthorpe Castle

If you were expecting a visit from your in-laws you might get a duster out, run a vacuum cleaner round the house and plump the cushions. In Tudor times things were rather different – especially for aristocrats, and particularly when the in-law in question was King Henry VIII.

The tale which is usually told about Grimsthorpe Castle (*inset*) is that it was built in haste by Charles Brandon, the Duke of Suffolk, in anticipation of a visit by Henry in 1541. It sounds like an apocryphal story, for a house had stood at Grimsthorpe for many years before the Duke set to work; but it has its roots in the truth.

The first building at Grimsthorpe was a Cistercian abbey founded near the lake in 1147. Early in the 13th century a castle was added nearby – today it surves as King John's Tower, the oldest part of Grimsthorpe Castle, with walls seven feet thick. Then the Duke of Suffolk set about enlarging the castle – 'of a sudden', according to one observer – to be sure of the approval of his royal brother-in-law.

Charles Brandon came by Grimsthorpe in a roundabout way. In 1516 Henry VIII gave the manor to the tenth Lord Willoughby de Eresby, whose family seat was near Spilsby. Lord Willoughby had married a Spanish lady-in-waiting to Catherine of Aragon, and Katherine, their daughter and heiress, married the Duke of Suffolk at the age of 16. She was the Duke's fourth wife; his third, Mary, had been the widow of Louis XII of France and also Henry VIII's sister.

Grimsthorpe has been called Lincolnshire's greatest and grandest country house, but chiefly by those cartographical nit-pickers who place Burghley House (p.8) beyond the Lincolnshire border. It achieved its present-day splendour in the 18th century, when Sir John Vanbrugh began work on rebuilding the entire castle. He didn't manage the feat, but he left his mark on Grimsthorpe, most notably in the form of its magnificent north front.

Memorials to the family whose home is Grimsthorpe Castle can be found a mile away, in the church at Edenham – all the way back to Robert Bertie, the first Earl of Lindsey, who was Lord Chamberlain and Lord High Admiral in the 17th century. With its dips and rises and its canopy of ancient trees, the country road which skirts Grimsthorpe and takes motorists to Edenham (*opposite*) is one of the most charming that Lincolnshire has to offer.

Bourne

Most of the primeval forest which once covered Britain is long vanished, but a patch of it survives just west of Bourne. Oak, ash and beech trees make up Bourne Wood, 2,000 years old and covering 400 acres; and it is accessible to the public, since it is managed by the Forestry Commission for conservation, coppicing, timber production and recreation.

What makes this surviving fragment of ancient woodland even more fascinating is the collection of 12 large-scale sculptures which can be viewed during the

course of a ramble through the woods. One of these is Simon Todd's sleeping woodcutter (*inset*), part of an unusual sculpture project established in 1991.

Bourne itself is not quite so old as the nearby woods; but it is much more ancient that it looks at first sight. The Romans brought their King Street and their Car Dyke canal through here, and in the Middle Ages the Arrouaisian canons (a sub-order of the Augustinians) founded an abbey in the town. The church of St Peter and St Paul, also known as Bourne Abbey church, is all that remains of it today.

The Elizabethan statesman William Cecil, Lord Burghley, was born in Bourne; the town was home to Robert Mannyng, who did much in the 14th century to standardise the English language; and it is reputed to have been the birthplace of Hereward the Wake, the swashbuckling Anglo-Saxon who fought a valiant last stand against the conquering Normans.

For a town with such a remarkable history, only a few buildings of great age survive. One of these is the Red Hall (*opposite*), a brick mansion dating from around 1610. It was sold to a railway company in 1860 and converted for use – bizarrely – as a booking office and stationmaster's house. The Hall was briefly in the limelight in 1996, when Granada Television used it as a location for their serialisation of Daniel Defoe's *Moll Flanders*.

Grantham

The chances are that you've heard of Grantham for one of three reasons: (1) Margaret Thatcher was born here, (2) the young Isaac Newton went to school here and observed his falling apple at nearby Woolsthorpe, and (3) Grantham was once dubbed the most boring place in Britain by a particularly ungenerous radio programme.

Natives of this south Lincolnshire town, which grew prosperous first as a staging post on the Great North Road and later as a centre for heavy industry, argued at the time that the 'boring' tag was never deserved. Although Grantham suffered badly at the hands of short-sighted 1960s town planners, who tore the heart out of much of the handsome Georgian town, the old town hall in St Peter's Hill was one of the happy survivors. An elegant building of brick and stone built by William Watkins in the late 1860s, it was converted by the district council into the Guildhall Arts Centre and theatre in 1991 (*inset*).

Now that the Premier Restaurant (Baroness Thatcher's childhood home) is no longer in business, Grantham's most visited landmark must be St Wulfram's church, well known for its soaring, slender spire – at 272 feet not quite as tall as St James's in Louth or St Botolph's in Boston, but a fine sight nevertheless. In the shadow of this ancient church are the nooks and crannies which show Grantham as it used to be: Vine Street, for example, (*opposite*) with some of its handsome brick houses dating back to the 18th century.

Back in the High Street are the vestiges of Grantham's glorious coaching past. One is the George Hotel, praised by Dickens in *Nicholas Nickleby* but now a shopping centre. The other is the famous and much older Angel and Royal Hotel, with its ornate 15th-century façade – one of the grandest English pre-Reformation inns. It was here in 1483 that Richard III signed the death warrant of the Duke of Buckingham, and here in 1633 that Charles I stayed as a guest. Today, by contrast, travellers to and from London shoot past on the A1 or on the east coast intercity main line; and to them Grantham is no more than a name on a signboard.

Harlaxton Manor

Harlaxton Manor – grandiloquent, overblown and utterly beautiful – is a testament to two Lincolnshire people: to George de Ligne Gregory, who pulled down the original manor in the 1830s and replaced it with this eccentric, magnificent pile (*opposite*), and to Mrs Violet Van der Elst, an ordinary woman with an extraordinary fortune who bought Harlaxton a hundred years later and saved it from dereliction.

No one knows for sure why Mr Gregory enlisted the architects Anthony Salvin and William Burn to create this phenomenal building – a mish-mash of styles, perhaps, or a breathtaking Victorian fusion of the best parts of England's architectural heritage, depending on your point of view. Mr Gregory was an established country gentleman whose family had lived at Harlaxton since the 17th century; but he had no heirs to inherit his awe-inspiring house. Our best guess is that he built Harlaxton simply to outdo his neighbours at Belton House, Stoke

Rochford Hall and Belvoir Castle, the last of which was extensively refurbished in 1825.

The story of Violet Van der Elst sounds almost as improbable. She was born Violet Dodge in Surrey in 1882, the daughter of a coal porter and a washerwoman, and after starting work as a scullery maid she became a successful businesswoman by developing Shavex, the first brushless shaving cream. By the end of the 1930s, now married to the Belgian Jean Van der Elst, she had amassed a huge personal fortune and earned notoriety from her vocal campaigns against capital punishment.

It was in 1937 that Mrs Van der Elst heard about Harlaxton Manor for the first time. The house boasted 100 bedrooms and 427 acres of parkland, but it had been neglected and was virtually derelict. In the desperate hope of saving it from demolition, agents advertised it for sale in the national press, and Mrs Van der Elst paid £90,000 for it.

The new owner's first acts were to rename the place Grantham Castle and to forbid shooting on the estate. By now a Labour politician who was to stand three times (unsuccessfully) for election to the Commons, Violet Van der Elst promised to preserve the grounds 'as a sanctuary for the dear birds and the wild creatures'. She then set about restoring the interior of her new home.

In 1959 Violet Van der Elst moved to a flat in Knightsbridge, her fortune almost spent. In 1965 the act abolishing the death penalty was passed, thanks in large part to her tireless campaigning; and a year later she died, penniless, friendless and obscure. Her memory lives on, however, at Harlaxton.

The Lincoln Cliff

In every direction Lincolnshire is cut off from the rest of the world: to the north by the river Humber, to the south by the Wash, to the east by the North Sea and to the west by the Lincoln Cliff. Stand at the crest of this long ridge, looking east, and the county of Lincolnshire slopes gently down, towards the marsh in the north, to the wolds further south, and finally to the fens. To the west, meanwhile, the land drops suddenly away – down to Gainsborough, to Nottinghamshire and to the broad plain of the river Trent.

The Lincoln Cliff goes by many names: it is also the Lincoln Edge, and south of Lincoln itself it is the Lincoln Heath. This narrow spine of limestone rises at Winteringham on the south bank of the Humber and runs southward for about 70 miles, through the iron and steel centre of Scunthorpe, through Lincoln (where it bears the castle and the cathedral on the hilltop) and on towards Stamford in the south-west.

Much of Lincolnshire has been unkind over the centuries to its builders – there was not much in the way of raw materials to be found in the watery fen and marsh that formed the east and south – but the Lincoln Cliff makes up for that. Our stone trail begins with Lincoln Cathedral itself, built chiefly in the 13th century of native limestone; and a journey south from the city along the picturesque A607 road will take the traveller through the heart of the Stone Belt.

Here mellow villages of warm limestone and pantile follow in rapid succession as one travels south: Harmston, Coleby, Navenby, Wellingore, Welbourn, Leadenham, Fulbeck, Caythorpe, and on towards Grantham; then the motorist must make a detour to avoid the A1 and follow instead the country road which leads on through more glowing stone pleasures: Boothby Pagnell, Bitchfield, Corby Glen (or turn off and explore Edenham and Grimsthorpe). And the road leads finally to Stamford, the pièce de résistance and arguably the most handsome stone town in all England.

Welbourn (*opposite*) lies below the line of the Cliff on the site of a 12th-century castle which is no more. It is also the birthplace of Field-Marshal Sir William Robertson, who rose to command all British forces during the First World War. Just three miles to the south is Fulbeck (*inset*), home for centuries to the Fanes of Fulbeck Hall and, uniquely, to two medieval village crosses.

To select just two of the Cliff's delights is to do the Stone Belt an injustice. All around are churches, halls and cottages built of native stone – in this part of the world everything is a delight to the eye.

Lincoln Cathedral and Minster Yard

'No gem in England's diadem shines more brightly,' reckoned Arthur Mee in his 'King's England' volume on Lincolnshire. 'Certainly not one of our cathedrals – not even Salisbury or Durham – is outwardly more striking.'

In penning his own admiration of Lincoln's glorious cathedral, Nikolaus Pevsner touched on one of the reasons for its grandeur: 'Apart from Durham,' he wrote, 'there is no English cathedral so spectacularly placed as Lincoln.' For Lincoln Cathedral towers above the ancient Roman and medieval city, dominating the picturesque old quarter, and its three grand towers perched on the crest of the hill can be seen by travellers from all directions as they approach Lincoln.

It is the third largest cathedral in England, and for its artistry and amazing scale it is arguably the finest. When it was first begun around 1072 by Remigius, England's first Norman bishop, it replaced a Saxon minster, and although an earthquake destroyed much of the Norman building in 1185, the magnificent west front survived.

Most of what tourists come to see today was begun in 1192 in the Early English style by Bishop Hugh of Avalon and completed about a hundred years later. It is a fantastic concrete expression of faith, whose ambition and execution is frankly breathtaking; to the people of Lincoln, of course, it is sacrosanct.

In 1995 the prospect of funding from the National Lottery led some in the city to call for the spires which originally topped the cathedral's three towers to be rebuilt. The central spire was destroyed by a storm in 1548 and the two on the west towers were considered unsafe and taken down in 1807. In view of the ongoing £750,000 which is spent each year on maintaining the cathedral in its present condition, however, the idea of restoring the spires was soon forgotten.

Our photographs show the west front of the cathedral from Castle Hill (*opposite*) and some of the handsome houses in Minster Yard, in the shadow of the great Gothic church (*inset*).

Newport Arch and the Stonebow

To live in Lincoln during the Roman occupation in the 1st century AD was to be an important person indeed. Soon after their invasion of Britain the Romans chose Lindon (a Celtic name meaning pool or marsh) as the site for their northernmost fortress, and by AD 90 Lindum had become Lindum Colonia, one of only four *colonia* established in Britain and therefore an imperial town of great importance.

Two major Roman roads – the Fosse Way and Ermine Street – met in Lincoln, and the commanding position of the *colonia* on top of the hill made it an important strategic location. The Roman city could be entered by four gates, and part of one of them survives to this day – Newport Arch (*opposite*), the northern gateway at the end of Bailgate. Between the 1600s and 1800s the other three gates either collapsed or were demolished.

The original gateway on this site would have been built of timber, but in the 3rd century it was dismantled and rebuilt in stone, with two stone towers flanking an arched stone tunnel. What survives today is only the inner wall of the gateway, but it is the oldest archway in England still used by road traffic on a daily basis.

A fragment of the first Roman south gate survives in Steep Hill (p. 38), but as Lindum Colonia grew in size, so newer gateways had to be added. The new Roman south gate stood in the High Street on the present-day site of the Stonebow (*inset*), which is its medieval replacement. Richard II ordered the rebuilding of the original Roman gate in 1390, but the work was not finished until 1520. The Stonebow has since been much renovated, especially in the 19th century. Inside is Lincoln's Guildhall, with the council chamber directly over the main arch, and the city's civic insignia. The Mote Bell on the roof bears its casting date of 1371 and is believed to be the oldest bell in England.

Steep Hill and Lincoln Castle

You can drive up the hill to the oldest and most interesting parts of Lincoln, but you ought to walk – not simply for the good of your health, but so that you may boast afterwards that you have conquered Steep Hill (*inset*).

Today Roman Ermine Street forms Lincoln's long, straight High Street, and beyond the Stonebow it becomes first The Strait and then Steep Hill, a cobbled lane whose gradient is so demanding that a handrail is provided for those who need it. Steep Hill leads the visitor into the splendours of uphill Lincoln – all boutiques, bookshops and *chocolateries* – and past some of the oldest houses (12th- and 13th-century) in the county.

Once at its summit, take a breather and admire the views from Castle Hill – not a hill at all, but a small square between the Norman castle to the west and the Gothic cathedral to the east. Two years after the Battle of Hastings William the Conqueror ordered the demolition of 166 mansions to make way for his new fortification, where today there is much to see: 14th-century Cobb Hall, whose roof was used for hangings until 1868; the part-Norman, part-14th-century Observatory Tower; and the Lucy Tower, named after Countess Lucy (a hereditary constable, or governor, of the castle).

Visitors to Lincoln Castle (*opposite*) can also tour the more recent prison, built on the castle green enclosure in 1787 and enlarged by the Victorians. The prison chapel is fascinating in its sadistic design: rows of cubicles were built so that felons could see the preacher but not their fellow inmates – 'a unique and terrifying space', Pevsner called it.

The Lincolnshire Show

Wherever there is farming you will find a farmers' show – a busman's holiday for those who earn their living from the land to justify a few days off by telling themselves they're really at work.

The Lincolnshire Show, staged annually in June on its own showground at Grange-de-Lings, north of Lincoln, has been a welcome diversion for the region's farmers for two centuries. The first Lincolnshire Agricultural Society was formed in 1796, but it was not until 1799 that some of its members first got around to showing off their livestock and competing for prizes.

That competitive spirit still lies at the heart of the modern Lincolnshire Show (*opposite*), though some of the judging criteria have altered somewhat since that first event 200 years ago. Instead of offering a prize for 'the labourer in husbandry who has brought up the most numerous family without parochial assistance', the judges are nowadays more concerned with the quality of the pedigree sheep, pigs, cattle and horses which are paraded around the show ring.

When Lincolnshire farmers first started putting their handiwork on display, the sheep and the pig were the county's staples. Today the growing of crops has pushed livestock farming into second place, but some of the old-style Lincolnshire breeds still survive to be admired on show day. Lincolnshire Longwool sheep (*inset*) and Lincoln Red cattle have both increased in number after a period of decline, although breeds such as the Lincolnshire Curlycoat pig will, sadly, never be seen again.

Livestock judging is not the only attraction at the Lincolnshire Show, of course – around 80,000 people visit the event over two days, and only a fraction of those are farmers. To keep them amused the Lincolnshire Agricultural Society lays on all manner of entertainment, from trade exhibits, crafts and conservation displays to showjumping, parachuting, falconry and sheepdog trials. It may no longer be the farmers' day out that it once was, but today the Lincolnshire Show is undoubtedly the county's most significant annual event.

Woodhall Spa

The poet Sir John Betjeman described Woodhall Spa as an 'unexpected Bournemouth-like settlement in the middle of Lincolnshire'. But Woodhall owes its air of Edwardian gentility more to the likes of Barnsley than Bournemouth, for it was during the search for coal hereabouts that curative mineral water was discovered. And that sealed the fortunes of Woodhall Spa (*inset*).

The story of John Parkinson is detailed elsewhere in this book, in the section on Old and New Bolingbroke (p.48). Around 1821 he sank a shaft in Woodhall in the vain hope of finding coal to power his new factory eight miles away in New Bolingbroke. But the only coal brought up from the shaft was the coal which the workmen took down with them in their pockets in order to prolong the project. Before long the 1,000-foot shaft was abandoned and allowed to fill with water.

While Parkinson went bankrupt another man took advantage of the situation. The local squire, Thomas Hotchkin, used the water from the shaft to ease his gout, and others in Woodhall found it a useful cure for rheumatism and skin ailments. A pump room and bath house were built and the water was drawn off into a brick-lined bath to treat the 20 or 30 patients who were visiting daily by 1841.

The railway made Woodhall Spa accessible to more visitors, and by the beginning of the 20th century a new garden-city plan drawn up for the town included a hospital, 23 shops and two luxury hotels. In Woodhall's Edwardian heyday the golf course, the Teahouse in the Woods and the concert pavilion were added. The pavilion is now a charming and unique cinema (*opposite*), the Teahouse is still open for business, and since 1996 the golf course has been the site of the headquarters of the English Golf Union, the governing body of English amateur golf. Today Woodhall Spa is also home to two of Lincolnshire's best known hotels – the Petwood and the Golf.

The only amenity which Woodhall Spa no longer has is a spa. It began to decline after the First World War but revived somewhat in 1948, when the new National Health Service gave it a role as a rheumatic and orthopaedic clinic – though drinking the spa water had been abandoned in 1930. In 1983 the spa baths were finally closed after the well collapsed.

Elsewhere in the town are two tributes to British military endeavour: Waterloo Wood, planted after the battle in 1815 by Colonel Richard Elmhirst and set off by a bust of Wellington on a stone obelisk; and the Dambusters' memorial to the men of 617 Squadron who dropped the 'bouncing bombs' on German dams in 1943 and whose officers' mess was in the Petwood Hotel.

Tattershall

The village of Tattershall stands, it can fairly be said, at the geographical heart of Lincolnshire. An ancient place studded with historical fragments, it is dominated today by the 15th-century brick tower of the castle (*opposite*) built by Ralph, Lord Cromwell, Lord High Treasurer of England and for many years the power behind the English throne.

Preserved and cared for now by the National Trust, the surviving keep was once just part of a bigger complex of towers, halls and outbuildings – all constructed by Lord Cromwell. But the castle didn't last long: Ralph's namesake Oliver Cromwell began the process of destruction, and by the end of the 17th century it was owned by a family who had no desire to live in it. The 20th century almost brought about its absolute demise; for the salvation of one of England's medieval treasures Tattershall has to thank the Marquess Curzon of Kedleston.

Between 1912 and 1914 Curzon spent a personal fortune of almost £60,000 on securing and restoring Tattershall Castle, and in a final act of munificence he bequeathed it to the nation when he died. His generosity, and the lasting impression he made on Tattershall, echoed the good work done in the village five centuries earlier by Ralph, Lord Cromwell, whose legacy lives on.

The village of Tattershall was not to be merely Cromwell's showy and impressive home; it was to be rebuilt as a seat of learning and an important place of worship. The Collegiate Church of the Holy Trinity, one of Lincolnshire's greatest Perpendicular churches, was founded alongside Cromwell's college, only a forlorn fragment of which survives today. And in the shadow of the church stands a row of almshouses – the Bede Cottages – which Cromwell rebuilt in 1440 under licence from Henry VI. The cottages (*inset*) have been much renovated since – the last time in 1967 – and must be a delightful place in which to live today.

Horncastle

Once the saying was 'Horncastle for horses'. This attractive market town (*opposite*) midway between Lincoln and the coast, on the border between wold and fen, was renowned for its August horse fair – judged in early Victorian times to be the biggest in the whole world.

Today the saying ought to be 'Horncastle for antiques', since the town is now deservedly famous as the antiques centre for eastern England; there are over 60 independent antiques dealers in Horncastle (*inset*), and collectors and buyers make a beeline for the place from as far away as continental Europe and the United States.

To the Romans Horncastle was Banovallum – 'the walled place on the river Bain', and an important fortress of which some fragments survive. Later the Anglo-Saxons had an even more precise name for their fortified home: Hyrnceastre, or 'the castle in the corner between the two rivers' (the Bain and the Waring). The richness of the farmland hereabouts gave Horncastle a prosperity which was augmented in 1230 by Henry III, who instituted a weekly market that survives to this day.

St Mary's church, with its bulky tower and its odd little spire, is built of the characteristic local greenstone, and the oldest parts of it probably date from the 13th century. Inside are clues to the decisive role which Horncastle and nearby Winceby played in the English Civil War. In 1643 Cavaliers and Roundheads clashed at the Battle of Winceby; the Cavalier Sir Ingram Hopton almost took Oliver Cromwell's life on the battlefield, but ultimately Hopton himself was slain, and after the defeated Royalists had been chased to Newark, Cromwell rode back to Horncastle and arranged for his enemy to be buried in St Mary's church.

The 13 scythe blades which can also be seen inside St Mary's are said by some to have been used in the Battle of Winceby, but there is no proof of this. What is certain, however, is that Cromwell spent the night in a house in West Street, since demolished, which stood next-door to the present-day Cromwell House.

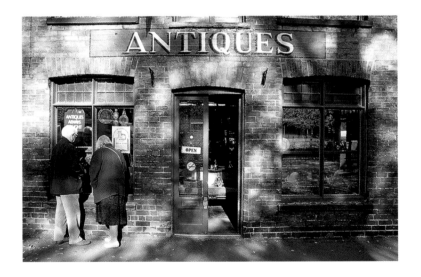

Old and New Bolingbroke

Few villages which share the same name can present such a contrast as Old and New Bolingbroke: one home to an ancient, tumbledown castle in the southern wolds, the other an elongated fenland community on the road known locally as the 'seven-mile straight'.

What links the two villages is the unbridled – and ultimately thwarted – ambition of the 19th-century visionary, John Parkinson. The son of a local land agent, Parkinson fixed on the idea of buying up newly drained fenland in the hope of a later rise in land prices. One of his early purchases was the medieval market town of Old Bolingbroke in the foothills of the wolds; in 1813 Parkinson transferred the weekly market to the site of his new city along the road that had recently been built between Frithville and Revesby.

Parkinson's plan was to use the road and the nearby navigable drain for transportation to and from his new textiles factory, which would be driven by coal from his

mine at Woodhall. In no time New Bolingbroke was thriving, with its own brickworks, corn windmill, brewery and maltings, market hall and a rather extravagant curved terrace of Georgian houses. As one correspondent wrote in 1824, 'New Bolingbroke has sprung up as if by magic in the heart of the fens.'

However, the success story was to turn sour. Parkinson borrowed heavily during the 1820s for investment, but the inaccessibility of his new town and the failure of his engineers to find coal at Woodhall made New Bolingbroke an impossible dream. In 1826 most of the town was put up for sale, and by the end of that year Parkinson was bankrupt. To visit New Bolingbroke today is to view the remains of what might have been: the market hall, the grand Crescent (*inset*) and the Victorian church are all evidence of once bright hopes which have long since dimmed.

The history of Old Bolingbroke is very different, but equally fascinating. Here a castle was built in the 11th century by William de Roumare, the first Norman Earl of Lincoln. Two centuries later John of Gaunt married his cousin Blanche of the House of Lancaster, whose property included Bolingbroke. In 1367 the couple had a son at Bolingbroke, a boy who grew up to be crowned Henry IV.

The castle (*opposite*) is in ruins today, though 20th-century excavations have given us a better idea of what it once must have looked like. Built of soft Spilsby sandstone, Bolingbroke Castle was always destined to fall down, and its final end came during the English Civil War when Roundhead troops dismantled it. The gatehouse was the last part to collapse, in 1815.

Tennyson Country

I loved the brimming wave that swam
Thro' quiet meadows round the mill.
The sleepy pool above the dam
The pool beneath it never still.
The meal sacks on the whiten'd floor
The dark round of the dripping wheel,
The very air above the door
Made misty with the floating meal.

Lovers of the poetry of Alfred, Lord Tennyson will be familiar with these lines from 'The Miller's Daughter', and those who know the southern Lincolnshire Wolds will recognise the setting as Stockwith Mill (*inset*), a place the poet knew well when he was a young man.

Alfred Tennyson was born at Somersby on 5th August 1809, the fourth son of the Reverend George Tennyson, rector of Somersby and Bag Enderby. He grew up to become a literary giant of the Victorian era and the greatest English poet of his age.

That part of Lincolnshire where Tennyson grew up – where the wolds first rise up out of the vast fen and amble north through places with such odd names as Hagworthingham, Mavis Enderby and Ashby Puerorum – is beautiful and as yet undiscovered. It has been known as 'Tennyson Country' for at least a century, but notwithstanding the appeal of its narrow, wooded valleys, its leafy lanes and its connections with the poet, this corner of the county remains unspoiled (*opposite*).

There is no World of Tennyson Experience to be found here, and you cannot buy a Tennyson tea towel or a Tennyson spice rack, even for ready money. For those with the patience to seek it out, however, the waterwheel at Stockwith Mill was restored to working order in 1981; and here, too, is a little permanent exhibition which will tell you all you need to know about Lincolnshire's most famous literary son.

Gunby Hall

Imagine how grave the threat of defeat by Nazi Germany must have seemed during the darkest days of the Second World War – so grave that the Air Ministry planned to bulldoze Gunby Hall (*opposite*) near Spilsby to make room for a longer runway at nearby RAF Steeping!

The plans were amended – thankfully – but only after the squire of Gunby, Field-Marshal Sir Archibald Montgomery-Massingberd, had brought his considerable influence to bear on the king. (He had until recently been Chief of the Imperial General Staff.) The runway at RAF

Steeping was indeed extended for use by Lancaster bombers, but its line was redrawn by a few inches and Gunby was saved.

The Field-Marshal was fighting to preserve not only a splendid three-storey William and Mary house and its beautiful gardens (*inset*), but also the ancestral seat of the Massingberds which had been in his family for two and a half centuries. The hall was built by Sir William Massingberd, the second Baronet, in 1700, according to the dated keystone on the west doorway: not one of Lincolnshire's grandest houses – 'a mason bricklayer's rather than an architect's design', thought Pevsner – but certainly one of the most lovable.

Gunby even made an impression on no less a person than Alfred, Lord Tennyson, Lincolnshire's poet laureate; he described it as 'an English home … all things in order stored, a haunt of ancient peace', words which he wrote out by hand and which now hang framed in the library.

The National Trust assisted in the negotiations which led to the preservation of Gunby Hall, and by way of thanks Sir Archibald and his wife gave their beloved home to the nation in 1944. It is now looked after by a Lincolnshire couple who moved in as tenants in 1967 and who open the hall and its serene gardens to the public on Wednesday afternoons.

The RAF in Lincolnshire

The link that binds the Royal Air Force with Lincolnshire was forged in the heat of conflict. The Royal Flying Corps used airfields at South Carlton, Kirton-in-Lindsey and Elsham in the First World War, and when the Second World War was at its height, Lincolnshire was home to 46 RAF stations. Lincolnshire became known as Bomber County, and the famous Dambusters of 617 Squadron launched their bombing raids on the dams of the Ruhr from Scampton.

Many of those airfields are now defunct, of course, but the RAF still thrives in some of them. Huge AWACS aircraft fly in and out of Waddington, south of Lincoln; the famous Red Arrows aerobatic team is now based at RAF Cranwell, north-west of Sleaford; and since 1986 enthusiasts have visited Coningsby, on the fringe of the fens north of Boston, to see the aircraft and crew of the Battle of Britain Memorial Flight.

Formed in 1965, the Red Arrows were initially based in the Cotswolds; now they are yellowbellies in red flying suits: a team of pilots flying nine Hawk jets at air shows and displays all over the world. Their home is noteworthy, too: Royal Air Force College, Cranwell (*inset*), built of stone-dressed red brick by Sir James Grey West in 1931, is far more elegant than your average RAF station. Its best-known landmark, the splendid dome and columns of the college chapel, was added in 1962.

Visitors to RAF Coningsby come from far and wide not for the buildings but for what's inside them. For this is the home of Britain's last flying Lancaster bomber, an aeroplane whose evocative drone can be heard overhead hereabouts throughout the summer. This special flight is best known as a trio: the Lancaster is usually seen in harness with a Spitfire and a Hurricane. But the Battle of Britain Flight actually comprises a Lancaster, two Hurricanes and four Spitfires as well as a Dakota.

There is even one airfield, long abandoned by the RAF, where memories of wartime endeavour are kept alive by local people. Brothers Fred and Harold Panton run the Lincolnshire Aviation Heritage Centre at East Kirkby, where their pride and joy is Lancaster NX 611 'Just Jane' (*opposite*) – not yet airworthy, but still a magnificent sight.

Wainfleet

Had George Bateman not decided, more than a century ago, to give up farming and try his hand at brewing instead, people outside Lincolnshire might never have heard of Wainfleet. True, this is by no means a famous place, but to those who know their beer, its name has a certain sanctity.

The brewery buildings of George Bateman and Son (*inset*) now include a disused windmill at Salem Bridge, whose tower serves as the company's symbol; and it is this landmark which visitors most often associate with Wainfleet, a fascinating town which has long lived in the shadow of Skegness, its neighbour five miles up the road.

But there's much else to see besides in Wainfleet, and a leisurely atmosphere in which to see it now that a bypass road has taken the holiday traffic out of the centre of town. Wainfleet was originally settled by the Anglo-Saxons as a place where they could take their wains (wagons) over the *fleot* which is now known as the river Steeping, and over the centuries it has prospered as both a market town and a river port.

William Patten, who became Bishop of Winchester and Lord Chancellor of England, was born here in 1395, and while he is best remembered as the founder of Magdalen College, Oxford, he never forgot his home town. Believing that 'Grammar is the mother of all science', Patten built a free grammar school for Wainfleet in 1484. The school continued to receive pupils until 1933, and now it is home to Wainfleet's museum and library.

Elsewhere in Wainfleet there is curious architecture of another sort – most notably Barkham Street (*opposite*), which looks for all the world like a terrace of town houses for London gentility rather than a row of dwellings for simple fenland folk. The trustees of the Bethlam Hospital in London built it in the 1840s, following architect's plans that had already been used to build an identical terrace in Southwark – the result is pleasing, but somewhat out of kilter with the rest of the town.

Skegness

For millions of holidaymakers the familiar symbol of 'sunny Skeggy' has always been the 'Jolly Fisherman' (*opposite*) – that splendid, ruddy-faced character with his sou'wester, boots and cheery smile who has enticed tourists to the east coast of Lincolnshire since 1908. But in actual fact he could very easily have found fame advertising some other seaside resort, rather than Skegness, with his jolly demeanour.

The artist John Hassall had no particular town in mind when he painted his 'Jolly Fisherman', but the Great Northern Railway Company paid £12 in 1908 to link the image with Skegness on one of their posters – and it was the GNR who came up with the now famous recommendation that 'Skegness is so bracing!'

Fifteen years later, when the spread of the motor car was causing a downturn in the numbers of holidaymakers travelling to Skegness by train, the London and North-Eastern Railway had Hassall update his poster by moving the fisherman to the left and adding the famous Skegness pier in the background. The original artwork for this new poster was discovered in a shed in Essex in 1995 and sold at auction for almost £6,000.

Built in 1881, the pier at Skegness always seemed cursed with bad luck, and after suffering the indignities of a fire, a shipping accident and a severe storm, most of it was washed away in 1978. But there's plenty left at Skegness to keep the tourists coming in by the thousand – not least the miles of wide, sandy beaches with which this part of the Lincolnshire coast is blessed (*inset*).

For centuries Skegness was just an obscure fishing village, and it was only at the end of the 18th century that the fashion for sea-bathing brought a reason for expansion. By the early part of the 19th century two hotels were open, catering for the well-to-do visitors who came to Skegness for the supposed health benefits of salt water and fresh air.

The advent of cheap rail travel for the working classes in Victorian times transformed Skegness from a well-heeled health resort into a holiday destination that everyone could afford. And Billy Butlin did his bit for the area in 1936 when he opened his first holiday camp a few miles up the coast at Ingoldmells. Knobbly knees competitions, 'Hello campers!' and the Jolly Fisherman; where else could we be but in Skegness?

The Lincolnshire Coast

Lincolnshire's coastline may be best known for the popularity of Skegness (p. 58), but it is not all sandy beaches and donkey rides. From the docks of Grimsby to the silty expanses of the Wash (an inland sea which extends from just south of Skegness round to Hunstanton in Norfolk, covering 183,000 acres at high tide), the character of this coast varies enormously.

Much of it is wild and inhospitable – one of few such places left in the country, it could be argued. Apart from

anything else, visitors have to watch out for the three bombing ranges where the RAF carry out their practice runs. There is not much fun to be had for the children either in some of the remoter parts of the Lindsey Marsh, or on the mudflats of the Wash; and precious few people visit Donna Nook in the north to bother the colonies of grey seals which breed on the beaches in early winter.

The Lincolnshire coast is a natural habitat for both common and grey seals. In 1988 a deadly virus reduced seal numbers in the Wash from around 5,000 to about 2,000, but the population is now on the increase once more. It's also one of the best places in the UK for watching seabirds. The coastal areas (the picture *opposite* was taken at Freiston) are an important feeding-ground for wading birds which fly south from October onwards – the best vantage points for ornithologists are on the banks of the Humber and around the Wash.

If you fancy a change from the garish attractions of Skegness, then the Gibraltar Point National Nature Reserve (*inset*) is only a short drive away. The 200,000 people who visit the reserve every year make it Lincolnshire's second most popular tourist attraction, after Lincoln's cathedral and castle. A remote area of sand dunes enclosing salt marshes, the reserve is now administered by the Lincolnshire Trust for Nature Conservation, which monitors the tens of thousands of birds that migrate through the area every year.

The Wolds

Anybody who has ever dismissed Lincolnshire as 'flat and boring' should be sent on a tour of the Lincolnshire Wolds. Begin at Keal Hill near Spilsby in the south, where the church perched on the hillside affords a glorious view of the fenland panorama below; continue north and west through the quiet green hills and valleys of the southern wolds; and press on, via the wild, remote road known as the Caistor High Street, dropping down if you fancy into one of the undiscovered wooded valleys to visit the villages of Normanby-le-Wold, Claxby, Walesby, Binbrook or Stainton-le-Vale (*opposite*).

Lincolnshire's wolds are a continuation of those low hills which tumble down from East Yorkshire: serene and unspoiled, they run for about 40 miles from the Humber Bridge down to Horncastle. And their appeal lies just as much in their quiet beauty as in the fact that they're virtually unknown to outsiders.

When wool brought prosperity to the market towns hereabouts, the wolds were home to countless thousands of sheep; nowadays cash crops are more profitable, and the recent introduction of oilseed rape and linseed has added an extra dimension – gaudy splashes of yellow, pale seas of blue – to the summer landscapes in this part of Lincolnshire.

The Lincolnshire Wolds offer so much to explore that it's hard to know where to start. Perhaps at Brocklesby, where the first Lord Yarborough planted three million trees in the 19th century; Pelham's Pillar commemorates that fact, although architecturally Brocklesby's gem is the classical mausoleum based by James Wyatt on the temples of Vesta at Rome and Tivoli.

Or you can pull on your walking boots and hike through the wolds. The Viking Way is a marked footpath opened in 1977 which runs all the way from the Humber Bridge in the north to Oakham in Rutland, and it takes in some of the best wolds scenery along the way. Follow the example of thousands of ramblers before you and pause for a breather at All Saints' church in Walesby above Market Rasen, once redundant but now reopened and known to all who pass by as the Ramblers' Church (*inset*).

Cadwell Park and Market Rasen

Despite the best efforts of Lincoln City, Grimsby Town and Scunthorpe United, Lincolnshire is not a county particularly well known for its sporting successes. But two locations in the county are firmly on the sporting map: the Cadwell Park motor-racing circuit near Louth (*inset*) attracts spectators from far and wide, and Market Rasen is known throughout the land for its horse racing (*opposite*).

In 1926 a certain Mansfield Wilkinson purchased land at Cadwell, in the heart of the Lincolnshire Wolds, which he considered perfect for rough shooting. But it was his son, Charles, who saw a quite different potential: the land would be ideal for motorcycle racing. The first three-quarters of a mile of broken chalk track was laid in 1934 around the old manor house.

The Second World War put a temporary end to racing, but by 1952 the circuit had been concreted, surfaced with tarmac and extended to a mile and a quarter. In 1961 it was extended again to its present length of two and a quarter miles. Cadwell Park was swallowed up by the Brands Hatch Leisure Group in 1987, but the wooded circuit still retains its rural Lincolnshire charm – an odd counterpoint to the roar of the motorcycles as they flash by.

In the 19th century, racing at Market Rasen took place just twice a year: there was a spring meeting featuring the prestigious steeplechase, and an autumn meeting to mark the beginning of feast week. By the 1870s the spring steeplechase had settled into the calendar on Easter Monday, and that tradition has survived to this day.

The Market Rasen races have had five different homes since the sport was formally introduced here in 1859, but they now seem certain to remain at their present home just outside the old market town, off Legsby Road, with the charming Willingham Woods in the background. Many a racing enthusiast has echoed the words of Norman Jackson in his poem 'The Races':

> Come, get your gallygaskins on
> An' off to Market Rasen.
> There will be good sport annon
> Fower them as puts theer shillings on
> Ower sticks at Rasen.

Louth

Few towns can have aged with such good grace as Louth, a place characteristic of Lincolnshire's modest, unassuming but infinitely charming market towns. There is nothing spectacular here – only mellow Georgian houses of red brick and pantiles, and an intriguing maze of streets (*opposite*).

Nothing spectacular, that is, except for St James's church (*inset*) – 'one of the most majestic of English parish churches', in Pevsner's view. At 295 feet, its spire is the tallest parish church spire in England. And yet it does not dominate the surrounding countryside in the way that the churches at Boston and Grantham do, since Louth lies in a fold in the hills; and from some directions the sight of magnificent St James's comes as something of a surprise.

An old verse once advised 'Boston for business, Louth for learning', and even today one can sense a certain air of culture about the town: Louth has a reputation as a centre for the arts, theatre and music which is the envy of many other towns its size. It also retains its ancient market, given by King Edward VI in a charter of 1551 to the grammar school which is now named after him. Sadly, nothing much remains of the Cistercian abbey which first brought wealth to Louth. The monks came originally from Fountains Abbey in Yorkshire to Haverholme near Sleaford, and when they found that place too swampy for their liking they moved again, in 1139, founding a new abbey a mile east of Louth. It flourished until the Middle Ages, when the Black Death brought about its demise.

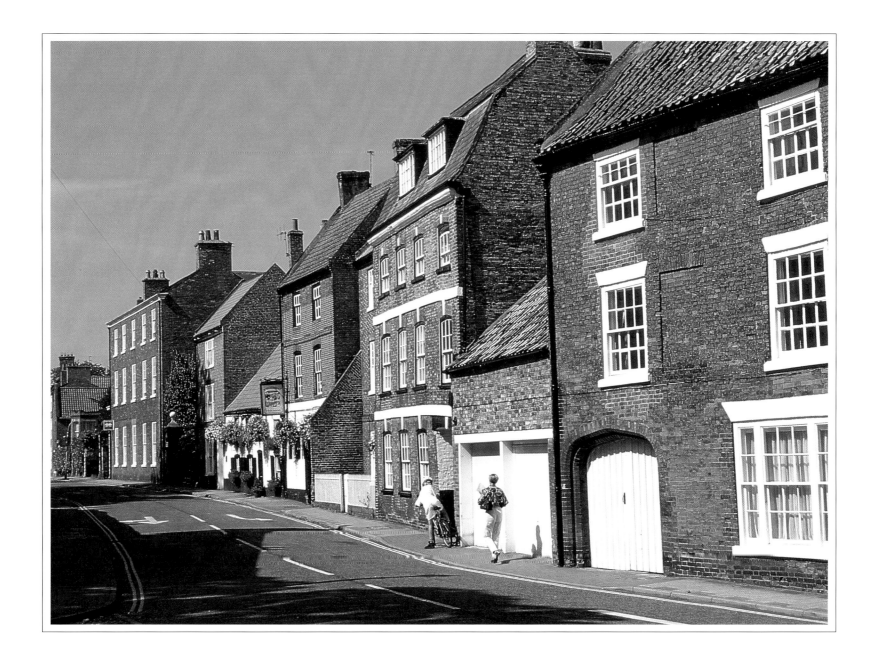

Cogglesford Mill and Alvingham Mill

In the days before the advent of sliced white and malted granary from the local supermarket, bakers relied on the elements for their flour: locally grown wheat was ground for them in mills powered either by wind or by the flow of running water.

Nowadays working watermills are a rarity indeed, but Lincolnshire has a handful of them which are open to visitors. One of these is Cogglesford Mill in Sleaford (*inset*), built around 1750 and particularly rare in that most mills in a town setting have long since been demolished. The existence of a mill on the site can be traced back as far as 1230, and the survival of the present building reflects the historical importance of watermills in the area: the Domesday survey of 1086 recorded 18 between Sleaford and nearby Ruskington.

After more than a century of use Cogglesford Mill closed in 1885, faced with competition from the big, industrialised mills of the Victorian era, and fell into disrepair. The virtual drying-up of the river Slea which once gave it life was a further indignity. But grade two listed-building status saved it from destruction, and in 1990 the mill was gifted to the local council, who had restored and reopened it by 1993. Work is also under way to restore the flow of the Slea to something like its former level, but for the time being milling is done with the help of a discreet electric motor.

Alvingham Mill (*opposite*) is older still – built in the 17th century – and was lovingly restored and opened to the public by its engineer owner in the 1970s. It stands north of Louth on the river Lud, not far from where the river is joined by the Louth Navigation Canal and led out to sea.

If you're in the area, you can see a local oddity by paying a visit to St Adelwold's church in Alvingham: it shares the same churchyard with St Mary's, the parish church of the next-door village of North Cockerington.

Gainsborough

The Victorian writer George Eliot was by all accounts delighted when she finally discovered Gainsborough (*opposite*) in 1859, and used it as the setting for her novel *The Mill on the Floss*. According to Beryl Gray, writing an appendix to a new edition of the book, 'her spirits must have soared when she and Lewes [her husband] arrived at Gainsborough and found the perfect St Ogg's'.

It must be said, however, that this ancient port on the river Trent has changed a good deal since Eliot's day. She described how 'the black ships – laden with the fresh-scented fir-planks, with rounded sacks of oil-bearing seed, or with the dark glitter of coal – are borne along to the town of St Ogg's, which shows its aged, fluted red roofs and the broad gables of its wharves between the low wooded hill and the river brink'. Planners destroyed Gainsborough's medieval street system in the 1960s, when the town looked destined to receive some of London's

population overspill. But two things remain untouched: Gainsborough's Old Hall, one of the finest examples of a medieval baronial manor house in England, and the tidal river Trent, which was so crucial to the setting of *The Mill on the Floss*.

It almost beggars belief that at one stage during the recent development of Gainsborough, someone mooted the idea of selling the Old Hall for car parking to cater for the expected increase in population; the town has the Friends of Gainsborough Old Hall to thank for its survival.

The oak-framed, brick-built hall which exists today was built in 1480 on the site of an older house. After its owners, the Hickman family, moved out of Gainsborough in the 18th century the hall was variously used as a factory, a theatre, a chapel, a pub and a tenement block. In 1952 it was leased to the Friends, and in 1970 it was given to the nation. Today it is owned by English Heritage, managed by Lincolnshire County Council and open to visitors.

What made Gainsborough so suitable as a basis for St Ogg's was the river Trent (*inset*); Eliot needed an inland port on a fast-flowing tidal river which had a history of flooding, and Gainsborough, with its annual Aegir, fitted perfectly.

At the spring equinox, when the tides are high and the river flow is small, a powerful wave named after Aegir, the Norse god of the sea, rises at the mouth of the Trent and drives a great volume of water back upstream. By the time it reaches Gainsborough it is a swollen and turbulent surge, tossing boats to and fro; it has claimed many innocent lives over the years. Despite recent dredging to mitigate the problem, the Aegir continues to command the respect of all those who use this part of the Trent.

Normanby Hall

A sprawling industrial conglomeration such as Scunthorpe is not at all what most people expect to find in quiet, rural Lincolnshire. Its transformation in the last century from five tiny villages into a town of some 70,000 inhabitants – for many years the beating heart of the UK steel industry – was rapid; and it all began in 1858, when the local squire went shooting with his friends on the common.

By that time the presence of iron ore in the land around the villages of Brumby, Frodingham, Ashby, Crosby and Scunthorpe had been all but forgotten, though the Romans had known it was there 2,000 years earlier. It was an unknown member of Lord St Oswald's shooting party whose eye was caught by the ironstone on the common, and the potential of the discovery soon dawned on the squire.

Scunthorpe grew out of all recognition, thanks to the new ironworks built by Lord St Oswald and his friend Sir Robert Sheffield of Normanby Hall. New railway lines stimulated the manufacture of iron for industry, and steel-making followed in 1890. Between 1900 and 1939 the population of Scunthorpe increased fourfold – for now the five villages had been swallowed and recast, iron-like, into one huge conurbation – and after the last war the borough council oversaw further rapid expansion.

The result, inevitably, was unattractive, but nearby Normanby Hall (*opposite*) is a more pastoral pleasure. The house was built between 1825 and 1830 by Sir Robert, whose family had moved to Normanby in the 16th century to escape the swampy Isle of Axholme to the west. Three hundred years later the Sheffields moved

again – this time to York – to flee the smoke and fumes of the new town they had created.

Today Normanby Hall and its surrounding country park (*inset*) are managed by North Lincolnshire Council and provide the public with a welcome oasis in an industrial desert. Two deer herds – one red, one fallow – were introduced onto the estate in 1964, and they continue to thrive.

Torksey Lock and Burton-on-Stather

To early man the river Trent must have presented a formidable barrier to communication on foot: rising in north Staffordshire, it flows through the heart of England and forms Lincolnshire's western border with Nottinghamshire. Finally, after a journey of over 170 miles, it meets the Ouse at Burton-on-Stather and forms the great river Humber, which then flows out to the North Sea.

To the Romans, however, the Trent was not an obstacle but a resource, and they increased its usefulness by linking the rivers Trent and Witham with a man-made canal. The Foss Dyke, which connects Lincoln with Torksey to the west, has been in use for over a millennium and is said to be the oldest navigable canal in the country (*inset*).

The Foss Dyke enables the sailor who so wishes to circumnavigate Lincolnshire: from Boston on the east coast it is possible to follow the Witham upstream as far as Lincoln and the Roman Brayford Pool, continue west and north along the Foss Dyke to Torksey, there join the Trent and sail north to Trent Falls, turn east along the Humber as far as the sea, then bear south back to Boston along the Lincolnshire coast.

In the past Torksey has been a place of some considerable importance: first a Roman port, then a site of strategic significance during the Danish invasions of Lincolnshire. The Domesday survey of 1086 recorded Torksey as the third largest town in Lincolnshire; it became a centre of trade where two priories were later founded and where Sir Robert Jermyn built his impressive Elizabethan mansion around 1560. The house was sacked by Royalist soldiers during the English Civil War and now only the west front survives, forlorn on the east bank of the Trent and looking for all the world like an abandoned film-set built for some Hollywood epic.

Burton on Stather (*opposite*) affords the best view of Trent Falls, where the Trent and the Ouse meet to form the Humber. 'Stather' here is the word for the landing-place, below the village and the Lincoln Cliff, for the ferry across the Trent to Garthorpe in the Isle of Axholme. On a clear day you can even see York Minster, 25 miles away.

Julian's Bower and the Humber Bridge

Separated by nine miles and at least 800 years of history, Julian's Bower and the Humber Bridge are two of Lincolnshire's great curiosities. Both are ingenious, and both have raised the same question in the minds of many: what on earth was the point?

Julian's Bower (*inset*) is a circular turf maze at Alkborough, 44 feet across and once thought to have been created by the Romans; Julus, son of Aeneas, is said to have brought a maze-like game to Rome from Troy, so that mazes are often called Troy Town, too. This maze was cut into the Lincoln Cliff overlooking the Trent Falls, where the rivers Ouse and Trent meet to form the Humber, and its survival is remarkable. A committee was set up in the 1950s to care for the maze, and a good deal of work was done by volunteers, who recut and rebuilt the spiral pathways.

How could they be sure of the plan of the original maze? By referring to the black and white stone replica set in the floor of Alkborough's 11th-century church. It

seems likely that the church is in fact older than the maze itself, and that those who originally cut Julian's Bower were monks who established an offshoot of Spalding's monastery here. We cannot know for sure what purpose the maze served, but the most likely explanation is that the monks used it as a penance, walking the paths over and over again with pebbles or dried peas in their shoes to remind them of their sin.

The purpose of the Humber Bridge (*opposite*) is far clearer. As long ago as the 1950s local government planners had a dream which they called 'Humberside', and in 1969 a government report recommended a bridge across the Humber to boost development in the region and to tie North and South Humberside together. Work began on the project in 1972 and the bridge was opened by Her Majesty the Queen in 1981; 470,000 tonnes of concrete and 44,000 miles of wire went into its construction.

When it opened to traffic, it was the longest-span suspension bridge in the world – 4,626 feet from the north to the south tower, beating San Francisco's Golden Gate Bridge by 400 feet – and on a clear day, with the sun glittering on the broad Humber, it is still a stirring sight. But it never stimulated trade between the north and south bank as it was supposed to, and the tolls have never come close to paying off the debt incurred by those who built it.

For 22 years the bridge was a symbol of Humberside, but then popular opinion got the better of that, too, and Humberside was abolished in 1996. So now the Humber Bridge is a symbol of something else: folly, perhaps; or engineering brilliance; or misguided planning. Everyone in this part of Lincolnshire has his own opinion.

Grimsby

If it weren't for Grimsby, we might never have seen the white beard of Captain Birdseye or heard the advertising slogan: 'As fresh as the day when the pod went pop!' For Grimsby – once the heart of the British trawling industry – has repositioned itself as Europe's 'Food Town'; it was here, on Lincolnshire's north-east coast, that Captain Birdseye (or someone close to him) invented the fish finger, and it was Grimsby which produced the first frozen pea. Though it is still officially Britain's number one fishing port, today Grimsby is home to only about 60 trawlers (*opposite*); earlier in the 1900s 650 vessels fished out of Grimsby dock.

Faced with the terminal decline of the fishing industry, Grimsby Fish Dock Enterprises invested over £14 million in a brand new fish market which opened in 1996. Now Grimsby is the UK's centre for buying, selling and freezing fish (*inset*), though only about a quarter of the catch is landed in the dock itself.

Fittingly, Grimsby takes its name from a poor Lincolnshire fisherman called Grim who (according to legend) rescued Havelok, a young Danish prince who had been put to sea in a boat following the murder of his father, King Birkabeyn. Grim raised Havelok as his own, and when the prince returned to Denmark and won back his kingdom, he bestowed a handsome reward on his rescuer. Grim used his new-found wealth to found the town which bears his name.

It is a workaday place, and not richly endowed with fine buildings; but one landmark stands out – the dock tower, designed in rather lavish style by J. W. Wild in imitation of the *palazzo pubblico* in Siena, and built in 1852 by J. M. Rendel. Dominating the docklands at a height of 309 feet,

the tower had a function when it was first conceived – to accumulate water pressure for working the locks, cranes and sluices of the docks. It remained in useful service for only 40 years, but since its retirement it has taken on a rather different role as the town's distinctive symbol.